152.4 Leghorn, Lindsay
Proud of our feelings.

$14.95

12)12·13

Proud of Our Feelings

written and illustrated by
Lindsay Leghorn

Magination Press • Washington, DC

To my big and little pals—
Barry, Riley, and Casey

Library of Congress Cataloging-in-Publication Data
Leghorn, Lindsay.
    Proud of our feelings / written & illustrated by Lindsay Leghorn.
        p.   cm.
    Summary: Priscilla introduces her friends, each of whom is feeling
and expressing a different emotion.
    ISBN 0-945354-68-1 hc – ISBN 0-55798-476-x pbk.
    1. Emotions in children—Juvenile literature. 2. Expression in
children—Juvenile literature. [1. Emotions.] I. Title.
BF723.E6L44   1995
155.4'124—dc20   95-1039
                                                                            CIP
                                                                            AC

Published by Magination Press
an Educational Publishing Foundation Book
American Psychological Association
750 First Street, NE
Washington, DC 20002

Manufactured in the United States of America

10 9 8 7 6 5 4 3

INTRODUCTION FOR
PARENTS AND PROFESSIONALS

This book has been designed to stimulate interaction about feelings between children and parents or other adults who care for them. The goal in doing so is to allow children to grow emotionally, knowing and trusting their own feelings. Too often we are told not to feel what we feel. We hear comments like "You shouldn't let that upset you" or "Oh, that didn't hurt you." In this way, our feelings are denied and our judgment and recognition of our own feelings can be lost.

There are no right or wrong, good or bad emotions or reasons for feeling. Feelings are a glorious part of our human condition. Reacting with understanding, interest and acceptance—rather than judgment—we encourage children to express and accept their own feelings. That self-acceptance is a basic stepping stone toward self-esteem and happiness.

Questions asked on each page of the story are offered as examples from which to expand. Children may respond by telling a story about a time they felt angry, or they may bring up other emotions not addressed in the book. Having children draw a new emotion, such as jealousy or embarrassment, can enhance their understanding and discovery. Playing a game of one person acting out a feeling while the other person guesses what it is can reduce the fear of emotional expression. Describing a situation and asking your child to imagine how someone might feel in that place can encourage empathy.

My hope is that children and parents together will discover, have fun with, and be proud of their feelings.

Hi! My name is Priscilla.
I have lots of friends.
We all have feelings
just like you.
  Come on . . .
   meet my friends.

Here's my friend Fred.

    Hi, Fred.

Fred is feeling friendly.
I can tell when he's feeling
friendly because he smiles
and tells people his name.

    What do you do when
    you feel friendly?

This is my friend Shelly.

    Hi, Shelly.

Oh, Shelly's feeling shy.

Meeting new people makes
her feel shy.

    What makes you
    feel shy?

Meet my friend Sandra.
        What's wrong Sandra?
Sandra's feeling sad.
She feels sad when her friends
don't listen to her.
        When was the last time
        you felt sad?

Here's my friend Hank.

Hello, Hank.

Hank's feeling happy.
His mom agreed to let him keep
the stray puppy he found.

What makes you
feel happy?

This is my friend Sid.
　　　Hey, Sid.
Sid's feeling silly.
He giggles and wiggles
and makes up goofy songs
when he feels silly.
　　　How do you act when
　　　you feel silly?

There's my friend Andy.
      Hello, Andy.
Andy's feeling angry.
He stomps his feet and
yells when he's angry.
      What do you look like
      when you're angry?

Meet my friend Connie.

  Hello, Connie.

Connie is feeling confident.
She feels confident when
she's riding her bike.

  When do you feel
  confident?

This is my friend Frida.
　　Hi, Frida.
Frida's feeling frustrated.
She slams her fist down
and lets out a loud grunt
when she feels frustrated.
　　How do you show
　　your frustration?

That's my friend Lonnie.
　Hi, Lonnie.
Oh, Lonnie's feeling lonely.
His best friend just
moved away.
　When have you
　felt lonely?

There's my friend Efrem.
Hey, Efrem.
Efrem's feeling excited.
He starts summer camp in a week
and can hardly wait.
What kinds of things
do you get excited about?

Here's my friend Scott.
Hi, Scott.
Scott's feeling scared.
He gets scared during
loud thunderstorms.
What things
scare you?

This is my friend Sara.
     Hello, Sara.
Sara's feeling safe and secure.
Her mom and dad are
holding her hands.
     What helps you feel
     safe and secure?

And here I am again — me, Priscilla — with my friends.

We are all proud of our feelings.

MAGINATION PRESS BOOKS

Breathe Easy: Young People's Guide to Asthma
Cat's Got Your Tongue? A Story for Children Afraid to Speak
Clouds and Clocks: A Story for Children Who Soil
Double-Dip Feelings: Stories to Help Children Understand Emotions
Gentle Willow: A Story for Children About Dying
Gran-Gran's Best Trick: A Story for Children Who Have Lost Someone They Love
Homemade Books to Help Kids Cope: An Easy-to-Learn Technique for
    Parents and Professionals
I Want Your Moo: A Story for Children About Self-Esteem
Ignatius Finds Help: A Story About Psychotherapy for Children
Into the Great Forest: A Story for Children Away from Parents for the First Time
Jessica and the Wolf: A Story for Children Who Have Bad Dreams
Julia, Mungo, and the Earthquake: A Story for Young People About Epilepsy
Little Tree: A Story for Children with Serious Medical Problems
Luna and the Big Blur: A Story for Children Who Wear Glasses
Night Light: A Story for Children Afraid of the Dark
Otto Learns About His Medicine: A Story About Medication for Hyperactive Children
The Potty Chronicles: A Story to Help Children Adjust to Toilet Training
Proud of Our Feelings
Putting on the Brakes: Young People's Guide to Understanding
    Attention Deficit Hyperactivity Disorder (ADHD)
The "Putting on the Brakes" Activity Book for Young People with ADHD
Russell Is Extra Special: A Book About Autism for Children
Sammy the Elephant and Mr. Camel: A Story to Help Children Overcome Bedwetting
Sammy's Mommy Has Cancer
Sarah and Puffle: A Story About Diabetes for Children
Scary Night Visitors: A Story for Children with Bedtime Fears
Tanya and the Tobo Man: A Story in English and Spanish for Children
    Entering Therapy
This is Me and My Single Parent: A Workbook for Children and Single Parents
This is Me and My Two Families: A Workbook for Children in Stepfamilies
The Three Birds: A Story for Children About the Loss of a Loved One
What About Me? When Brothers and Sisters Are Sick
Wish Upon A Star: A Story for Children with a Parent Who Is Mentally Ill
You Can Call Me Willy: A Story for Children About AIDS
Zachary's New Home: A Story for Foster and Adopted Children